CW00420707

THE STATUE OF LIBERTY:
The Story and Legacy
of a United States Icon

by Bill Wiemuth

HISTORYHIGHLIGHTS.COM PRESENTS

THE STATUE OF LIBERTY:
The Story and Legacy
of a United States Icon

by Bill Wiemuth

Published by
HistoryHighlights.com
Fascinating true stories in less than an hour.
For the curious mind without a lot of time.
— Online Multimedia Presentations —
— eBooks — Paperbacks — Audiobooks —

Visit HistoryHighlights.com
and sample our recent newsletters,
plus receive free books, video presentations,
and updates about new releases.

ACCOLADES

An incredibly important and fascinating saga in our nation's history, told by the master of US history storytelling.
– Trudy Cusack

My husband told me if he had attended a history class in high school given by someone like you, he probably would have gone on to school and become a history teacher.
– Joy Snider

Bill Wiemuth is able to do what so many historians cannot. He can take history and put it in a form that is not only enjoyable but makes you want more.
– David

Bill, your knowledge of the history of our country is second to none and your presentation of the material was entertaining as well as informative.
– Sally and Fred Burner

Bill's ability to entwine the river and history, and a bit of fun, really brought to life each event. The historical background on these issues was both interesting and educational.
– Lon and Kathy Willmann

CONTENTS

The Statue of Liberty under construction in France, courtesy of Wikimedia Commons.

INTRODUCTION

She towers 151 feet tall. She has a 420-inch waist. (That's 35 feet!) From ground level to the tip of her torch is 305 feet. Her index finger extends just over 8 feet. She wears 60,000 pounds of copper. She is adorned with a 9-foot crown accented with seven spikes to represent the seven oceans and the seven continents of the world, indicating the immensity of the universal concept she honors: Liberty.

On an island in New York harbor stands one of the world's most incredible sights: The awe-inspiring Statue of Liberty Enlightening the World. At her 1886 dedication, she stood as the tallest human-made structure in the world and the most remarkable statue ever constructed.

Standing in New York harbor since 1886, the statue has become an icon of liberty, the United States, patriotism, immigration, controversy, and much more. About 3.5 million people annually visit the statue and its museum.

But, also on Liberty Island, in the shadow of the symbol of America, stand two other clusters of bronze statues created by sculptor Phillip Ratner. One group represents the more than 12 million immigrants that were welcomed to America by Lady Liberty as ships arrived at the nearby United States immigration station at Ellis Island. The second group of statues commemorates five people who contributed greatly to the completion and legacy of the Statue of Liberty: A French politician, Edouard de Laboulaye; a French engineer, Alexander-Gustave Eiffel; a French sculptor, Frédéric Auguste Bartholdi; an American publisher, Joseph Pulitzer; and, an American poet, Emma Lazarus. With the support of hundreds of thousands of French and American citizens, they brought a remarkable concept to reality: A statue to embody the ideal of Liberty.

This is the story of visionary dreams, enormous struggle, the power of many, an unlikely international achievement in partnership between France and the United States, the precious concept of liberty, an icon of immigration, and a mighty feminine colossus named for her purpose: Liberty Enlightening the World.

Welcome to this History Highlights book sharing the story and legacy of the Statue of Liberty. My name is Bill Wiemuth and I am excited to share with you this amazing story about one of the great American icons.

If you have a curious mind, but not a lot of time, you have made the perfect decision to join me for this amazing story. If you love fascinating true stories of intriguing people and incredible events that shaped the history of the United States, then you are in the right place.

At HistoryHighlights.com, enjoy our FREE weekly newsletter with free eBooks, video presentations, and updates about our ongoing development of new eBooks, audiobooks, and multimedia programs! Learn more at HistoryHighlights.com.

A love of history grows into a thrilling passion. So, get ready to fall in love with history – again or for the first time. Experience wonder. Revel in these incredible tales of remarkable people and events that shaped – and continue to shape – the United States. Visit HistoryHighlights.com to explore great stories from history.

In this book, we will explore how the vision began for a colossal gift from the people of France to the people of the United States and the remarkable people, struggles, and drama that brought that vision to reality. Let us first explore a few elements of background to illuminate the spark of this grand vision and this remarkable chapter of history.

Get ready for a journey of discovery.

THE VISION

EDOUARD DE LABOULAYE

In the first few months of 1865, the United States Congress passed the 13th Amendment to abolish slavery and the union of the United States was preserved by the federal victory over the rebellion of the Confederated southern states.

Across the Atlantic, in Paris, Frenchman Édouard de Laboulaye was thrilled and inspired. Laboulaye was a professor, politician, writer, and anti-slavery activist. As a fervent admirer of the United States Constitution, Laboulaye wrote a three-volume work chronicling the political history of the United States. He had been a zealous advocate of the Union cause and the abolition of slavery, publishing histories of the cultural connections between the two nations. As the United States Civil War ended in 1865, he became president of the French Emancipation Committee to aid newly-freed slaves in the United States.

Laboulaye believed that the United States legislation to abolish slavery was a milestone that proved that justice and liberty for all was possible.

Laboulaye lived in a little village near the Palace of Versailles. At a dinner party, Laboulaye discussed the idea of presenting a statue representing liberty as a gift to the United States as a gesture of celebration and to help strengthen France's relationship with the United States.

One of Laboulaye's friends at that dinner party was sculptor Frédéric Auguste Bartholdi. The suggestion was a lasting one. Years later, Bartholdi remembered Laboulaye's words:

> *If a monument were ever built in America to celebrate the independence of the United States, it would be fitting that it be built by the united efforts of France and the United States, since they struggled together for American independence.*

The statue not only would commemorate the progress of freedom in the United States, but also illuminate the suppression of freedom France was enduring under the rule of Napoleon III. Laboulaye hoped that by calling attention to the recent achievements of the United States, the French people would be inspired to call for their own democracy in the face of a repressive monarchy.

Bartholdi wrote, "I will try to glorify the Republic and liberty over there in the hope that someday I will find it again here in France if it can be done."

AUGUSTE BARTHOLDI

Auguste Bartholdi was born on August 2, 1834, in Colmar, Alsace, France. He was a talented young man and studied art, sculpture, and architecture. At age 21, Bartholdi and some fellow artists visited Egypt to view the Sphinx and Pyramids of Giza. Bartholdi was enthralled by the massive artwork and their timelessness. He wrote:

> *We were filled with profound emotion in the presence of these colossal witnesses, centuries old, of a past that to us is almost infinite, at whose feet so many generations, so many*

million existences, so many human glories, have rolled in the dust.

Bartholdi's talent soon involved him in many projects. To sit at the northern entrance to the Suez Canal, he proposed to build an enormous lighthouse in the form of an ancient Egyptian female peasant, robed and holding a torch aloft. He called it "Egypt (or Progress) Carrying the Light to Asia." He drew inspiration from the legendary Colossus of Rhodes, an ancient bronze statue of the Greek god of the sun, Helios which stood more than 100 feet tall at a harbor entrance and carried a light to guide ships. Unfortunately, Bartholdi's Suez Canal project never came to fruition due to expenses.

According to Bartholdi, Laboulaye's alleged comment about the gift of a monument from France to the United States was not intended as a proposal, but it inspired Bartholdi. He later wrote, "The idea remained fixed in my memory."

But in July of 1870, France declared war on Prussia and any dreams of a large project were overshadowed by the Franco-Prussian War. Bartholdi became a major in the National Guard of the Seine. In the war, Napoleon III was captured and deposed. France lost the fight to protect Bartholdi's home province of Alsace, which was lost to the Prussians. However, a more liberal republic developed in France.

So, in 1871, Bartholdi and Laboulaye decided the time was right to discuss the monument idea with influential Americans.

On June 8, 1871, Bartholdi departed for America. Sailing into New York harbor provided a grand entrance to the United States. Bartholdi noticed an island situated at that harbor entrance and learned it was called Bedloe Island. He wrote, "I have found the admirable spot. It is Bedloe's Island, just opposite the Narrows which are, so to speak, the gateway of America."

His friend and mentor Laboulaye was well respected and renowned in the United States due to popular English translations of Laboulaye's series of books about the United States Constitution and another biography series about Benjamin Franklin. The letters of introduction provided by Laboulaye gained access for Bartholdi to many of America's brightest and most powerful people. Bartholdi even met President Ulysses Grant at Grant's summer home in Long Branch, New Jersey. Bartholdi discussed the ambitious project and Grant assured him that it would not be difficult to obtain a site for the statue.

Bartholdi traveled to Philadelphia and met with more of America's early leaders. He learned that Philadelphia would host an elaborate 1876 exposition to celebrate the nation's centennial. Bartholdi even discussed creating a large work for the event.

In Washington, D.C., he was thrilled to meet Massachusetts Senator and famed abolitionist Charles Sumner. Bartholdi was delighted that Sumner was a Francophile and his house was filled with French art and furnishings.

Sumner had been in the Senate for 20 years. In 1852 he gave his first ferocious speech in the Senate denouncing slavery. His bold opposition eventually led to South Carolina Democratic Representative Preston Brooks savagely beating Sumner on the Senate floor in May of 1856. Sumner was absent recovering for the rest of the year and returned to the Senate in 1857 for only a single day. With only brief and infrequent Senate appearances, Sumner traveled across Europe for much of the next two years, including extended stays in France. He and Laboulaye shared many of the same passions for liberty and the abolition of slavery.

By June of 1860, Sumner was back in the Senate and again vehemently denouncing slavery.

Bartholdi continued on to meet influential people in Boston and even visited Henry Wadsworth Longfellow. Bartholdi had met Longfellow's son Charles while traveling in Egypt.

Bartholdi wanted to see more of America. He learned that very few Americans had ever visited the west and that travel was rumored to be difficult. Undeterred, toward the end of August 1871, Bartholdi departed westward from New York's new Grand Central depot.

He visited Chicago, Illinois, and then proceeded on to Omaha, Nebraska. Occasionally, the train held for hours waiting for immense herds of buffalo to pass. In Utah, he visited Promontory Point to view the spot where the Central Pacific and the Union Pacific had connected the continent's first transcontinental railroad just two years earlier in 1869.

The west was dotted with just a sprinkling of rough towns. Salt Lake City seemed like an oasis in the wilderness. The majestic Mormon Temple could seat 8,000 people. After meeting the Mormon leader Brigham Young, Bartholdi wrote to his mother with amazement that Young had 16 wives and 49 children.

In California, Bartholdi disembarked the train to detour along a rough and dusty stagecoach journey to see the giant redwood trees. He arrived at nightfall at a crude inn but was led awestruck on a moonlight hike into a collection of trees 400-600 years old stretching up to 30 feet in diameter and 350 feet tall. Their oversized grandeur must have connected with Bartholdi's love of colossal beauty.

He proceeded to San Francisco and stayed until early autumn before making his return journey. Traveling back across Missouri, he wrote: "We cross for some time some superb forests. Autumn is giving them some ravishing color."

At St. Louis, Missouri, he marveled at the parade of Mississippi River steamboats. He stayed several days in Pittsburgh, Pennsylvania, and visited manufacturing facilities producing iron, steel, glass, and other products. He described the city's hundreds of furnaces and dense, hovering smoke.

When he returned to the nation's capital, Congress was in session and Senator Sumner introduced Bartholdi to many influential people around Washington.

Throughout his nationwide travels, Bartholdi continually promoted the idea of the monument and wrote to Laboulaye, "The ground is well prepared; only the spark will have to be provided by a manifestation on the part of France."

Sailing out of New York, he again envisioned a great statue standing on Bledsoe's Island. He wrote, "I am sure that it is right that on that island should rise 'Liberty Enlightening the World...It is exactly here that my statue should be erected—here, where people have their first view of the New World."

During Bartholdi's absence, France had endured a civil war and Paris was severely damaged. He and Laboulaye decided to wait before mounting a public campaign. Bartholdi continued to develop drawings and models for the concept. He also worked on several large sculptures designed to bolster French patriotism after the defeat by the Prussians.

In 1872, Bartholdi and Laboulaye founded the Franco-American Union in Paris to raise funds for the construction of their envisioned statue.

In 1875, Laboulaye proposed that the French finance the statue and the U.S. provide the site and build the pedestal.

Bartholdi's design ideas were coalescing. But he needed a model to help him develop the design. The following year while at a friend's wedding, he spotted a young woman with the body shape, posture, and arms that he envisioned. He learned that her name was Jeanne-Emelie and she worked as a seamstress assistant. Despite the difference in economic class, the two fell in love and she moved to Paris to model for him. However, he repeatedly could not summon the courage to reveal the relationship to his affluent mother.

FROM VISION TO REALITY

DESIGN

With the modeling help of Jeanne-Emelie, the design concept for the statue began to develop. Liberty, derived from Libertas, the goddess of freedom was widely worshipped in ancient Rome. A Liberty figure already adorned most American coins of the time. A representation of Liberty already crowned the dome of the United States Capitol Building.

Bartholdi wished to give the statue a peaceful appearance and chose for the figure to hold in her right hand a torch, representing the enlightenment needed to achieve liberty. In her left hand, she would hold a tablet inscribed in Roman numerals to commemorate the July 4, 1776 date of the U.S. Declaration of Independence.

As a tribute to the nation's recent abolition of slavery, a broken shackle and chain would lay at the statue's feet as she steps forward in progress.

Her head would be crowned with a halo of seven rays to represent liberty expanding to the seven seas and the seven continents.

Bartholdi wrote of his vision:

The surfaces should be broad and simple, defined by a bold and clear design, accentuated in the important places. The enlargement of the details or their multiplicity is to be feared. By exaggerating the forms, in order to render them more clearly visible, or by enriching them with details, we would destroy the proportion of the work. Finally, the model, like the design, should have a summarized character, such as one would give to a rapid sketch. Only it is necessary that this character should be the product of volition and study, and that the artist, concentrating his knowledge, should find the form and the line in its greatest simplicity.

Bartholdi's friend and mentor, architect Eugène Viollet-le-Duc designed a brick pier to anchor the statue and to which the metal skin would be anchored. After consultations with the metalwork foundry Gaget, Gauthier & Co., copper was chosen for the skin. The copper sheets could be heated and then shaped with wooden hammers.

Bartholdi planned for the final statue to tower just over 151 feet.

PROGRESS

The project progressed in increments for the next several years in a symbiotic partnership of fundraising, construction, and promotion. Each element empowered the others. Promotional events fueled fundraising which enabled construction which supported additional promotion.

Philadelphian John W. Forney visited Paris on a goodwill tour promoting the upcoming 1876 United States Centennial Exposition. During Bartholdi's tour of America, they had discussed the possibility of Bartholdi designing a large fountain for the Exposition. But when Forney saw Bartholdi's model of Liberty, he wanted it completed for display at the Centennial. Forney assisted with fundraising efforts and the project advanced.

By 1875, France's postwar economy was recovering and its politics somewhat stabilized. The increasing interest in the United States Centennial Exposition in Philadelphia led Laboulaye to decide it was time to seek public support.

A "birthday" celebration for Liberty was held on November 6, 1875, with a formal dinner at Louvre Hotel. They proposed the project as a partnership between France and the United States. France would fund the statue if the Americans would provide a location and pedestal for her. The Franco-American Union would coordinate fundraising. With the announcement, the statue was given a name, "Liberty Enlightening the World."

Laboulaye arranged events designed to appeal to the rich and powerful, including a special Paris Opera performance on April 25, 1876, that featured a new cantata by Charles Gounod, the composer of the opera "Faust."

Initially focused on the elites, the Union was eventually successful in raising funds from across French society. The project grew to be a matter of national French pride funded by the public and not with governmental money.

Schoolchildren and ordinary citizens contributed — including 181 French municipalities and more than 100,000 individual donors. A French copper industrialist donated 128,000 pounds of copper for the project.

Two hundred bronze castings of the statue's model were sold as well as tickets to view the construction activity. The French government authorized a lottery. In the next several years, hundreds of thousands of francs were raised.

At the Gaget and Gauthier shop in the winter of 1875, Bartholdi explained his idea to a team of assembled workers: From the approved four-foot plaster model, they would measure and enlarge to an eight-foot model, then expand again to a 36-foot model. Those pieces would again be meticulously measured and quadrupled in size. More than 1,200 marks would be measured three times each. They then would build a custom wooden frame to fit every curve of the plaster. Workers would overlay copper on the wooden frames and hammer the pieces into shape. The hundreds of pieces would be assembled like a puzzle and attached with rivets to a metal frame like a skin being attached to a skeleton.

Work progressed on the arm, hand, and torch to display at the United States Centennial Exhibition.

PREVIEW PIECES

In May 1876, Bartholdi traveled to the United States as a member of a French delegation to the Centennial Exhibition. The large and ornate "Fountain of Light and Water" he had designed was a popular attraction. After the exhibition, the fountain was relocated and still stands as a centerpiece of the United States Botanic Garden in Washington, D.C.

While Bartholdi awaited shipment of the statue's massive arm and torch, he traveled to New York City and on July 4 he first visited Bedloe's island with a crew to take preliminary measurements. Isaac Bedloe had acquired ownership of the island in 1667. It later served as a quarantine and hospital. The United States government acquired the island in 1800 and a coastal fortification was constructed. During the Civil War, it operated as a Union recruiting station.

After surveying the island, Bartholdi visited the studio of his friend John La Farge. In a moment of heartache, Bartholdi confided to John and John's wife Margaret about his love for Jeanne-Emelie, the woman who had served as the model for the statue, and his inability to tell his mother of his desire to marry. Margaret suggested he send for Jeanne-Emelie and that they marry in the United States. Bartholdi mailed Jeanne-Emelie the suggestion the following morning.

On August 12, 1876, the completed torch-bearing arm finally arrived from France in pieces packed into 21 large crates. The project was transported to Philadelphia, assembled, and debuted for the Centennial Exhibition's New York Day celebration on September 21. Crowds were mesmerized and enjoyed climbing to the balcony of the torch to view the fairgrounds.

After the Exhibition, the pieces also were displayed in Madison Square in New York City until 1882 to assist in fundraising.

The Statue of Liberty Arm on display at the 1876 Philadelphia Centennial Exposition. Courtesy of Wikimedia Commons.

Thrilled with Bartholdi's romantic offer, Jeanne-Emilie traveled to America and the two were married on December 15, 1876, at the La Farge's home in Newport, Rhode Island.

In early January 1877, Bartholdi assisted with setting up the American Committee for the Statue of Liberty to coordinate fundraising in the United States for the pedestal. Committees were formed in New York, Boston, and Philadelphia.

Bartholdi and his new bride traveled back to Paris. His mother awaited the new couple and quickly grew fond of Jeanne-Emilie. They soon learned that on March 3, 1877, on his final full day in office, President Grant signed a joint resolution to accept the statue when it was presented by France and to select a site for it. President Rutherford B. Hayes soon committed to the Bedloe's Island site that Bartholdi had proposed.

With fundraising progressing, Bartholdi concentrated on completing the statue's enormous head. During the construction, the Paris workshop was visited by former President Grant while visiting Europe in the autumn of 1877.

By June of 1878, the statue's head was moved on a cart by 12 horses through the city streets to be displayed to great acclaim at the Paris Universal Exhibition of 1878.

THE BEGINNING

As fundraising allowed, the work continued. Bartholdi's lead engineer became ill in 1879 and soon died. The following year, Bartholdi contracted Gustave Eiffel to design and build an enormous iron truss tower. Eiffel planned for the structure to flex and move slightly in winds or as the metal expanded in heat. He included two interior staircases for visitors to access the observation area in the crown. The statue would be completely constructed there in France, then disassembled and transported to the United States to be reassembled on Bedloe's Island.

The momentous project officially began on October 24, 1881, as United States Ambassador to France Levi Morton ceremoniously hammered in the first rivet to attach a copper plate onto the statue's big toe. (Eight years later, Morton would become United States Vice President to President Benjamin Harrison.)

The work continued on several segments simultaneously in a manner that often confused visitors. Some work was performed by coppersmith contractors as far away as southern France.

By the middle of summer in 1882 she was completed up to her waist and Bartholdi celebrated by inviting reporters to lunch on a platform built within the statue.

For portions of 1883, work stopped when it became apparent that America had raised no funds for a foundation and pedestal.

The project suffered a significant blow when Edouard de Laboulaye died on May 25, 1883. But a new highly-visible supporter took up the torch of advocacy. The French committee welcomed new chairman Ferdinand de Lesseps who had become famous as the project manager for the construction of the Suez Canal.

After a month-long United States exhibition raised $12,000, Bartholdi and his workers went back to work.

Piece by piece and day by day, the statue rose above Paris until fully constructed. A series of celebration dinners followed. Official announced that the French government would provide transportation for the statue to the United States.

In a ceremony on July 4, 1884, United States Ambassador Levi Morton received the formal presentation from Ferdinand de Lesseps. Guests climbed the 12 stories up 168 steps to the crown. As the statue towered over Paris for the following months, an array of dignitaries visited including 82-year-old author Victor Hugo. Hugo afterward wrote to Bartholdi with these insightful words, "Form to the sculptor is all and yet nothing. It is nothing without the spirit; with the idea it is everything."

Across the Atlantic, the United States completed construction of a 50-foot-thick foundation which was built at a cost of almost $100,000. The cornerstone for the massive pedestal was laid on August 5, 1884.

The statue remained intact in Paris as they waited for the Americans to make sufficient progress on the pedestal. Finally, in January 1885, workers began to disassemble, number, label, and crate the statue in preparation for her ocean voyage to America.

Many French were saddened to see her depart, so a group of wealthy Americans in Paris raised funds to have a 35-foot bronze cast of Bartholdi's studio model made to remain in Paris (where it is still on public display on an island in the Seine River).

TO AMERICA

By early May 1885, the statue was loaded into 214 crates and onto a special train of 70 cars. Many French citizens lined the streets to bid her a fond farewell and bon voyage. Loaded aboard the ship "Isere," Lady Liberty's vessel departed France on May 22 and endured 10 days of severe storms during her almost month-long ocean crossing.

When the "Isere" finally arrived in New York on June 19, 1885, some 200,000 people lined the docks and more than 100 vessels escorted the ship in from Sandy Hook to Bedloe Island. But the pedestal for the statue to be erected upon remained uncompleted. For the previous six months, the construction of the pedestal had repeatedly halted due to lack of funds. Work had restarted only a week before the cargo arrived. So, the Statue of Liberty was unloaded onto the island and sat waiting in her crates for more than a year.

UNITED STATES FUNDRAISING

Fundraising efforts in the United States to support the Statue of Liberty project proved difficult. The Panic of 1873 was an international financial crisis that led to an economic depression that persisted through much of the decade. As a result, the Liberty statue project was not the only such endeavor that struggled to raise money. The construction of the obelisk later known as the

Washington Monument sometimes stalled for years and ultimately required more than three decades to complete.

American committees took little action for several years. New York governor Grover Cleveland in 1884 vetoed a bill to provide $50,000 for the statue project. An attempt the following year to have Congress provide $100,000, sufficient to complete the project, also failed. By 1885, the committee had spent almost $180,000 and had less than $3,000 remaining. With the project in jeopardy, groups from other American cities, including Boston and Philadelphia, offered to pay the full cost of erecting the statue in return for relocating it.

On March 13, 1885, the press reported that work on the foundation would cease.

Publisher of New York's "The World" newspaper, Joseph Pulitzer, came to Lady Liberty's rescue. His mantra, he said, was "Publicity, publicity, publicity is the greatest moral factor and force in our public life."

Pulitzer wrote in a March 16, 1885, article:

We must raise the money! The World is the people's paper, and now it appeals to the people to come forward and raise the money. The $250,000 that the making of the Statue cost was paid in by the masses of the French people- by the working men, the tradesmen, the shop girls, the artisans- by all, irrespective of class or condition. Let us respond in like manner. Let us not wait for the millionaires to give us this money. It is not a gift from the millionaires of France to the millionaires of America, but a gift of the whole people of France to the whole people of America.

Nearly ten years ago the French people set about making the Bartholdi statue. It was to be a gift emblematic of our attainment of the first century of independence. It was also the seal of a more serviceable gift they made to us in 1776, when, bur for their timely aid, the ragged sufferers of Valley Forge would have been disbanded and the colonies would have continued a part of the British dominion. Can we fail to respond to the spirit that actuated this generous testimonial?...

It would be an irrevocable disgrace for the city of New York and the American Republic to see France send us this splendid gift without our having furnished simply a place to put it. There is only one thing to do – we must collect money.

The World is the people's paper, and it now appeals to the people to come forward and raise the money...Take this appeal to yourself personally...Give something, however little.

Thanks to Pulitzer's crusade, "The World's" campaign was so popular that by August 11, 1885, the newspaper collected just over $100,000 in donations to complete the pedestal. Roughly 125,000 people contributed and 80 percent of the total was received in sums of less than one dollar. In thanks, "The World" published the names of each person who donated (no matter its size), an act that also advanced the sales of Pulitzer's newspaper. A note with one donation read, "Enclosed please find five cents as a poor office boy's mite to the pedestal fund."

A group of children wrote, "We send you $1, the money we have saved to go to the circus with."

Alan Kraut, Professor of History at American University in Washington, D.C. put Pulitzer's effort in perspective:

The spirit of the democratization of the funding of the statue, I think, is what's important. Had they the will, a handful of New York millionaires could easily have funded that pedestal. But how much more appropriate to have the pennies of schoolchildren and the coins of people of very modest means — those who had been born in America and those that had come to America — to fund this statue. Now it really is a people to people endeavor.

As the donations flooded in, the committee resumed work on the pedestal. Bartholdi visited the United States again for three weeks in November of 1885 to assess the progress.

ONE HUNDRED THOUSAND DOLLARS!

TRIUMPHANT COMPLETION OF THE WORLD'S FUND
FOR THE LIBERTY PEDESTAL.

Story of the Greatest Popular Subscription Ever Raised in America—How the Republic Was Saved from Lasting Disgrace—An Event for Patriotic Citizens to Rejoice Over—A Roll of Honor Bearing the Names of 120,000 Generous Patriots—The Flags of France and the American Union Floating in Sisterly Sympathy—Over $2,300 Received Yesterday—The Grand Total Foots Up $102,006.39—A Generous Lady Pays $130 for the Washington Cent.

CONSTRUCTION

The foundation of Bartholdi's statue was laid inside Fort Wood, a disused army base on Bedloe's Island constructed between 1807 and 1811. After 1823, it had rarely been used. During the Civil War, it served as a recruiting station. The fortifications of the structure were in the shape of an 11-pointed star.

The statue's foundation and pedestal were aligned so that it would face southeast, greeting ships entering the harbor from the Atlantic Ocean.

The New York committee had commissioned architect Richard Morris Hunt to design the pedestal. In Hunt's original conception, the pedestal was to have been made of solid granite. Financial concerns forced him to revise his plans so the final design called for poured concrete walls, up to 20 feet thick, faced with granite blocks. The concrete mass was the largest poured to that time. With 56 million pounds of concrete and granite, when the pedestal was finally completed in April 1886, reassembly of the statue began.

The Statue of Liberty's pedestal under construction on Bedloe's Island in 1885. Courtesy of Wikimedia Commons.

The iron skeleton structural framework designed by Gustave Eiffel was erected within three months. On July 12, 1886, the first copper pieces were added with the first of the 600,000 rivets required to reassemble the statue. The rest of the Statue's elements followed without the use of scaffolding – all construction materials were hoisted up by steam-driven cranes and derricks.

Bartholdi had planned to put floodlights on the torch's balcony to illuminate it, but only a week before the dedication, the Army Corps of Engineers vetoed the proposal, fearing the light could impair ship navigation. Instead, Bartholdi cut portholes in the torch—which was covered with gold leaf—and placed the lights inside them. A power plant was installed on the island to light the torch and for other electrical needs.

As the statue was erected in 1886 it was the tallest structure in the world. Bartholdi wrote,

Colossus statuary does not consist simply in making an enormous statue. It ought to produce an emotion in the breast of the spectator not because of its volume but because its size is in keeping with the idea that it interprets and with the place which it ought to occupy."

The cost of building the statue and pedestal amounted to more than $500,000 which would exceed $10 million today.

DEDICATION

This 1886 painting by Edward Moran depicts the unveiling of the Statue of Liberty on October 28, 1886. Courtesy of Wikimedia Commons.

As the statue neared completion, an elaborate dedication ceremony was planned for October 28, 1886. Congress approved $56,000 to clean up the construction site and facilitate the ceremonies. Renowned landscape architect Frederick Law Olmsted supervised a cleanup of Bedloe's Island. Olmstead already had served as co-designer of Manhattan's Central Park and Brooklyn's Prospect Park. The American Electric Manufacturing Company donated a plant to power the statue's lights.

Just days before the unveiling, Bartholdi wrote that even though he was concerned about some of the lines, he felt proud. He wrote: "The dream of my life is accomplished; I see the symbol of unity and friendship between two nations—two great republics…it is a success. I believe that it will last until eternity."

October 28, 1886, was rainy, but the response was numerous and enthusiastic. A crowd estimated to contain up to one million people gathered along a five-mile parade route. The crowds cheered the 2.5-hour procession of some 20,000 parade participants. As the parade passed the New York Stock Exchange, traders threw ticker tape from the windows, beginning the New York tradition of the ticker-tape parade. "The World" newspaper noted, "the city was one vast cheer."

Dignitaries proceeded aboard ships to view a naval parade of more than 300 vessels before proceeding to Bedloe's Island.

The dedication ceremonies included such dignitaries as France's Ferdinand de Lesseps, New York Senator William M. Evarts (the chair of the American fundraising committee), and President Grover Cleveland. Bartholdi was called upon to speak, but he declined. Instead, he climbed to the torch to personally release a French flag that had been draped over the statue's face. A miscommunication of cues resulted in the flag being dropped early before President Cleveland had even spoken.

When Cleveland did speak, his remarks were well-chosen. He said:

The people of the United States accept with gratitude from their brethren of the French Republic the grand and completed work of art we here inaugurate. This token of the affection and consideration of the people of France demonstrates the kinship of republics, and conveys to us the assurance that in our efforts to commend to mankind the excellence of a government resting upon popular will, we still have beyond the American continent a steadfast ally.

We are not here today to bow before the representation of a fierce and warlike god, filled with wrath and vengeance, but we joyously contemplate instead our own deity keeping watch and ward before the open gates of America, and greater than all that have been celebrated in ancient song. Instead of grasping in her hand thunderbolts of terror and of death, she holds aloft the light which illumines the way to man's enfranchisement. We will not forget that Liberty has here made her home; nor shall her chosen altar be neglected. Willing votaries will constantly keep alive its fires, and these shall gleam upon the shores of our sister republic in the East. Reflected thence, and joined with answering rays, a stream of light shall pierce the darkness of ignorance and man's oppression, until liberty enlightens the world.

Due to the inclement weather, the dedication ceremony fireworks and torch lighting were delayed until days later.

The dedication of the Statue of Liberty received immense media coverage across the United States and internationally. Here are some sample newspaper headlines from the dedication's coverage:

The Colossal Statue Dedicated with Splendid Ceremony.

It was a fitting tribute to the sister republic's magnificent gift

An Army in the March—A Great Fleet on the Water.

Our President Greets the Representatives of France.

And a Million of our People Gather for the Notable Event.

The Rain Fell but Patriotism and Ardor Glowed Fervidly.

A Detailed Record of the Day and all its Ceremonies.

Bartholdi Witnesses the Crowning Glory of a Great Career.

"The World's" share in the Great Work Gracefully Acknowledged.

As Lady Liberty was dedicated, 21 years had passed since the dinner at Édouard de Laboulaye's where the statue's concept had first been discussed. Bartholdi had first visited New York 15 years earlier. A full decade had elapsed since the celebration of the United States Centennial.

After a telegraph alerted Bartholdi that his mother in France had become ill, he quickly departed. He left behind a magnificent legacy — a triumphant symbol as a touchstone reminder to a nation to preserve and cherish the preciousness of liberty.

Bartholdi did eventually return to visit his creation and advocate for her preservation and development. Bartholdi continued to design and create many more amazing projects. He even designed his own funeral monument and soon after it was finished, Bartholdi died on October 4, 1904. The Statue of Liberty Enlightening the World still stands as his most spectacular achievement.

HIGHLIGHTS OF A CENTURY

CONTROVERSY

Controversy regarding the statue began almost immediately. No members of the general public were permitted on the island during the ceremonies, which were reserved entirely for dignitaries. The only females granted access were Bartholdi's wife, Jeanne-Emilie, and Ferdinande "Tototte," the teenage daughter of Ferdinand de Lesseps. Even the wives of the American Committee were left to watch the proceedings from a boat anchored off Bedloe's Island. Officials stated that they feared women might be injured in the crush of people. The restriction offended area suffragists, who chartered a boat and got as close as they could to the island. The group's leaders made speeches applauding the embodiment of Liberty as a woman and advocating women's right to vote.

Other oppressed groups shared those feelings. Only 4 years earlier, the United States government had passed the 1882 Chinese Exclusion Act which prohibited Chinese immigration and prevented Chinese Americans from becoming citizens.

Shortly after the dedication, "The Cleveland Gazette," an African American newspaper, suggested that the statue's torch not be lit until the United States became a free nation "in reality." They wrote:

"Liberty enlightening the world," indeed! The expression makes us sick. This government is a howling farce. It

*cannot or rather does not protect its citizens within its own
borders. Shove the Bartholdi statue, torch and all, into the
ocean until the "liberty" of this country is such as to make
it possible for an inoffensive and industrious colored man to
earn a respectable living for himself and family, without
being ku-kluxed, perhaps murdered, his daughter and wife
outraged, and his property destroyed. The idea of the
"liberty" of this country "enlightening the world," or even
Patagonia, is ridiculous in the extreme.*

ADAPTIONS

Just after the turn of the century in 1900, the statue's
original dull copper color began to turn green due to the
oxidation of the copper skin. Repairs were considered,
but an Army Corps of Engineers study concluded the
statue was not being damaged.

The statue was administered by the United States
Lighthouse Board until 1901 and then by the Department
of War. Throughout World War I, Lady Liberty was the
last view of America for many departing soldiers and
their first view upon their return.

On July 30, 1916, the statue was damaged as German
saboteurs in nearby New Jersey detonated carloads of
explosives that were being shipped to the war efforts.

Also in 1916, Mount Rushmore sculptor Gutzon
Borglum was contracted to redesign the torch and much
of the flame's copper was replaced with amber-colored
glass.

That same year, Ralph Pulitzer – who had succeeded
his father Joseph as the publisher of New York's "The
World" newspaper – raised funds from more than 80,000
contributors for an exterior lighting system to illuminate

the statue at night. On December 2, 1916, President Woodrow Wilson pressed a telegraph key to turn on the lights.

In 1924 President Calvin Coolidge designated the statue as a National Monument. In 1933 President Roosevelt transferred the site and structure to the care of the National Park Service as part of the Statue of Liberty National Monument.

Liberty's lights were darkened during WWII but were reignited on May 8, 1945, in celebration of Victory in Europe Day.

In 1956, Bledsoe Island was formally renamed Liberty island and in 1965, nearby Ellis Island was added as part of the Statue of Liberty National Monument.

In 1966 the Statue of Liberty was added to the National Register of Historic Places. In 1984, Lady Liberty was designated a UNESCO World Heritage Site. The UNESCO "Statement of Significance" describes the statue as a "masterpiece of the human spirit" that "endures as a highly potent symbol—inspiring contemplation, debate and protest—of ideals such as liberty, peace, human rights, abolition of slavery, democracy and opportunity."

RENOVATION

In preparation for the statue's 1986 centennial, the statue underwent a series of assessments and renovations.

To fund the restoration efforts, President Ronald Reagan in May 1982 announced the formation of the Statue of Liberty–Ellis Island Centennial Commission, led by Chrysler Corporation chair Lee Iacocca. In a

September 1985 interview with "Guideposts" magazine, Iacocca discussed his involvement:

In 1921 my father sailed past Lady Liberty with his elderly mother and his new young bride at his side. They were greenhorns. They didn't know the language or customs. They were poor, except for two important resources: ambition and hope…

When you think about it, except for the American Indians. we're all immigrants or the children of immigrants: people who proudly brought their ethnic heritage —- culture, music, literature and cuisine —- to stir into the American melting pot.

For all of us, the Statue of Liberty and Ellis Island stand for American ideals: compassion, the dignity of labor, the chance to live abundantly, the fight for what's right, the freedom to worship as we please.

So that's why this son of Nicola and Antoinette Iacocca is beating the drum for Lady Liberty. And thanking God for the privilege of doing it.

The Statue of Liberty–Ellis Island Centennial Commission raised more than $350 million in donations to fund significant repairs and renovations to the statue in preparation for her centennial celebration.

Repairs were made to the copper skin and structural elements, and the torch was replaced with a replica of Bartholdi's unaltered torch with a flame covered in 24-karat gold. The iron support structure designed by Gustave Eiffel was replaced with ferralium, an alloy that bends slightly and returns to its original shape as the statue moves. The lighting was again upgraded. A grander entrance to the pedestal was framed by a set of monumental bronze doors. A modern elevator was installed, allowing guests with mobility challenges to access the observation area of the pedestal. An emergency elevator also was installed within the statue, reaching up to the level of the shoulder.

July 3-6, 1986, was designated "Liberty Weekend" and President Ronald Reagan presided over the rededication, with French President François Mitterrand in attendance.

Three decades later, Liberty Island again celebrated a major renovation as a new 26,000-square-foot Statue of Liberty Museum opened on May 16, 2019. The facility was made possible by more than $100 million in donations raised by the Statue of Liberty/Ellis Island Foundation. Their board fundraising chair Diane von Furstenberg said, "It was actually easy, because when you start to talk about her and what she represents, people somehow get moved."

Before the museum opened, only 20 percent of visitors had access to the interior of the monument where the statue's original torch was displayed and where the rich history of Lady Liberty was told in a small museum located within the pedestal. As the museum opened, Stephen Briganti, President and CEO of the Statue of Liberty-Ellis Island Foundation said, "Starting today, every visitor who comes to Liberty Island will have the opportunity to have a full museum experience, to learn about Lady Liberty's history and how She still shines as a beacon of hope for all people around the world."

For more than a century, Lady Liberty has stood as an iconic sentry for her nation despite visitation occasionally having been inaccessible due to renovations, security concerns, severe weather, and more. She began as a symbol of friendship between France and the United States and a celebration of the abolition of slavery. She has represented liberty, stood as an icon of the United States, and become a symbol for immigration.

Courtesy of Wikimedia Commons.

IMMIGRATION SYMBOL

The Statue of Liberty's development as an icon of immigration was dramatically impacted by its location, a poem, and presidential speeches.

ELLIS ISLAND

Located near Bedloe's Island in Upper New York Bay, the United States government in 1892 opened a federal immigration station on Ellis Island. For the next 62 years, until 1954, the facility served as the processing center for more than 12 million people immigrating to the United States. During the peak years of its operation from 1900 to 1914, about 5,000 to 10,000 people passed through the facility every day. The nearby Statue of Liberty often was the first thing those newcomers saw when arriving by ship.

THE NEW COLOSSUS POEM

Before the crates containing the disassembled pieces of Lady Liberty had ever departed France, poet Emma Lazarus had authored a poem that would become synonymous with the statue.

In 1883, Lazarus was asked to compose a sonnet for an art and literary auction to raise funds for the Statue's pedestal run by the American Committee for the Statue of Liberty. Lazarus was inspired by her experiences working with refugees and the plight of immigrants and thus included a new facet of liberty in her interpretation of what the statue could mean. The poem vividly depicts the Statue of Liberty as offering refuge to new immigrants.

After the auction, the sonnet appeared in Joseph Pulitzer's "The World" newspaper as well as "The New York Times" but the poem received little attention at the time.

It was not until 1901, 17 years after Lazarus's death, that friends of the poet, led by Georgina Schuyler, organized a civic effort to resurrect and promote the forgotten poem. Their efforts succeeded as the text of the poem was emblazoned on a commemorative bronze plaque which was affixed to the base of the statue in 1903. The plaque now is on display inside the Statue's pedestal and a replica resides inside the Statue of Liberty Museum.

The title of the poem and the first two lines reference the Greek Colossus of Rhodes, a famous sculpture alongside the harbor of Rhodes in the third century BCE.

"The New Colossus" by Emma Lazarus
Not like the brazen giant of Greek fame,
With conquering limbs astride from land to land;
Here at our sea-washed, sunset gates shall stand
A mighty woman with a torch, whose flame
Is the imprisoned lightning, and her name
Mother of Exiles. From her beacon-hand
Glows world-wide welcome; her mild eyes command
The air-bridged harbor that twin cities frame.

"Keep, ancient lands, your storied pomp!" cries she
With silent lips. "Give me your tired, your poor,

Your huddled masses yearning to breathe free,
The wretched refuse of your teeming shore.
Send these, the homeless, tempest-tossed to me,
I lift my lamp beside the golden door!"

FRANKLIN D. ROOSEVELT'S 1936 SPEECH

On October 28, 1936, a ceremony commemorating the statue's 50th anniversary was attended by dignitaries including the French Ambassador to America Andre de Laboulaye, the grandson of the statue's visionary supporter. President Franklin Delano Roosevelt's speech paid great tribute to the statue's evolution as an immigration icon and immigration as a central part of the nation's character. Following are some selections from Roosevelt's speech that day:

For over three centuries a steady stream of men, women and children followed the beacon of liberty which this light symbolizes. They brought to us strength and moral fiber developed in a civilization centuries old, but fired anew by the dream of a better life in America. They brought to one new country the cultures of a hundred old ones.

I think it has not been sufficiently emphasized in the teaching of our history that the overwhelming majority of those who came from the nations of the old world to our American shores were not the laggard, nor the timorous, nor the failures. They were men and women who had the supreme courage to strike out for themselves...They adopted this homeland, because in this home, in this land they found the home which the things they most desired could be theirs: Freedom of opportunity, freedom of thought, freedom to worship God. Here they found life, because here was freedom to live.

It is the memory of all these eager-seeking millions that makes this one of America's places of great romance. Looking down this great harbor, I like to think of the countless number of inbound vessels that have made this port.

I like to think of the men and women who...strained their eyes to the west for a first glimpse of the New World...They came to us speaking many tongues, but a single language, the universal language of human aspiration. How well their hopes were justified is proved by the record of what they achieved. They not only found freedom in the New World, but by their effort and devotion, they made the New World's freedom safer, and richer, more far-reaching, more capable of growth.

...It was the hope of those who gave us this statue and the hope of the American people in receiving it that the Goddess of Liberty and the Goddess of Peace were the same...And the richness of the promise has not run out. If we keep the faith for our day, as those who came before us kept the faith for their's, then you and I can smile with confidence into the future.

It is fitting therefore, that this should be a service of rededication, rededication to the liberty and the peace which this statue symbolizes. Liberty and peace are living things. In each generation — if they are to be maintained — they must be guarded and vitalized anew.

We do only a small part of our duty to America when we glory in the great past. Patriotism that stops with that is a too-easy patriotism— a patriotism out of step with the patriots themselves. For each generation, the more patriotic part is to carry forward American freedom and American peace by making them living facts in a living present. To that we can, we do, rededicate ourselves.

RONALD REAGAN'S 1986 SPEECH

A half-century after Roosevelt's speech, President Ronald Reagan echoed these themes during his July 3, 1986, speech as he presided over the "Liberty Weekend" rededication. Following are selections from Reagan's speech:

While we applaud those immigrants who stand out, whose contributions are easily discerned, we know that America's heroes are also those whose names are remembered by only a few. Many of them passed through this harbor, went by this lady, looked up at her torch, which we light tonight in their honor.

They were the men and women who labored all their lives so that their children would be well fed, clothed, and educated, the families that went through great hardship yet kept their honor, their dignity, and their faith in God. They passed on to their children those values, values that define civilization and are the prerequisites of human progress. They worked in our factories, on ships and railroads, in stores, and on road construction crews. They were teachers, lumberjacks, seamstresses, and journalists. They came from every land.

What was it that tied these profoundly different people together? What was it that made them not a gathering of individuals, but a nation? That bond that held them together, as it holds us together tonight, that bond that has stood every test and travail, is found deep in our national consciousness: an abiding love of liberty. For love of liberty, our forebears -- colonists, few in number and with little to defend themselves -- fought a war for independence with what was then the world's most powerful empire. For love of liberty, those who came before us tamed a vast wilderness and braved hardships which, at times, were beyond the limits of human endurance. For love of liberty, a bloody and heart-wrenching civil war was fought. And for love of liberty, Americans championed and still champion, even in times of peril, the cause of human freedom in far-off lands.

"The God who gave us life," Thomas Jefferson once proclaimed, "gave us liberty at the same time."

But like all of God's precious gifts, liberty must never be taken for granted. Tonight, we thank God for the many blessings He has bestowed on our land; we affirm our faithfulness to His rule and to our own ideals; and we pledge to keep alive the dream that brought our forefathers and mothers to this brave new land.

On this theme the poet Emma Lazarus, moved by this unique symbol of the love of liberty, wrote a very special dedication 100 years ago. The last few lines are ones we know so well; set to the music of Irving Berlin, they take on tonight a special meaning.

[At this point, a choir sang the last few lines from Lazarus'
poem "The New Colossus."]

We are the keepers of the flame of liberty. We hold it high
tonight for the world to see, a beacon of hope, a light unto
the nations. And so with joy and celebration and with a
prayer that this lamp shall never be extinguished, I ask that
you all join me in this symbolic act of faith, this lighting of
Miss Liberty's torch.

At the end of the concert and the fireworks, Supreme
Court Chief Justice Warren Burger officiated a ceremony
broadcast by satellite to naturalize new citizens across the
country. Via the broadcast ceremony and various local
events, some 38,000 new citizens representing 109 foreign
nations were sworn in that day. Justice Burger said:

Our Constitution is a unique remarkable instrument. Two
hundred years ago, it operated to unleash the talents,
energies and abilities of every individual who came
here...People were meant to be free. The statue symbolizes
not only our freedom but also the Constitution that
guarantees that freedom and has guaranteed that freedom
for 200 years.

CLOSING

My name is Bill Wiemuth and I thank you for joining me for this History Highlights book about the Statue of Liberty.

I certainly hope you have enjoyed learning from this presentation. I also hope you are developing a fascination for history. There is so much to explore, learn, and enjoy. I know you will savor every moment of it.

At HistoryHighlights.com, explore an ever-growing collection of books, audiobooks, and 200+ video presentations offering you fascinating true stories you can enjoy in less than an hour. Enjoy a free trial at: https://historyhighlights.vhx.tv/

Please tell your friends and family about History Highlights. And connect with us online to enjoy FREE eBooks, audiobooks, and video programs in our weekly history newsletter at HistoryHighlights.com.

We've spotlighted fascinating true stories such as the international intrigue and secret deals that enabled The Louisiana Purchase. A two-book set highlights the incredible adventure of the Lewis and Clark Expedition. Another book illuminates the remarkable role of the Mississippi River. Or explore the impact on the Civil War of the Union's Anaconda Plan, intended to cripple the South's economy by controlling the Confederate coastline and waterways. The story of the first steamboat to travel down the Mississippi River is an adventure where everything that could go wrong did go wrong. But that riveting drama changed the U.S. economy and history forever. Another great adventure story follows the Oregon Trail pioneers' incredible journey to the Pacific Northwest. Our Mark Twain and the Mississippi River presentation shares how the river impacted Twain's life, career, and writings. And much, much more.

PLEASE – A QUICK REVIEW.

Your review of this book is one of the primary ways we expand to find a new and growing audience of readers. Please leave your review in just a few seconds at this link:

https://tinyurl.com/StatueReview

Thank you so much!

We have many more books available to explore and enjoy in a variety of formats including eBooks, paperbacks, and audiobooks. We also have a site offering more than 200 history video presentations. Please stay in touch with us with our free weekly HistoryHighlights.com newsletter. Enjoy free books, video presentations, and special insights. Preview samples and join our journey of discovery at HistoryHighlights.com.

TO LEARN MORE

Following are just a few suggestions of resources to continue your exploration of the history and significance of the Statue of Liberty. Enjoy your journey of discovery!

— —BOOKS— —

The Statue of Liberty Enlightening the World
by Frédéric Auguste Bartholdi

Bartholdi and the Statue of Liberty
by Willadene Price

Liberty Rising: The Story of the Statue of Liberty
by Pegi Deitz Shea

— —VIDEOS— —

Ken Burns 1-hour PBS episode available at PBS website:
https://tinyurl.com/y9db9or3

— —ONLINE— —

Excellent National Park Service sites
https://www.nps.gov/stli/index.htm

https://www.nps.gov/articles/liberty.htm

https://www.nps.gov/stli/learn/historyculture/index.htm

ABOUT THE AUTHOR

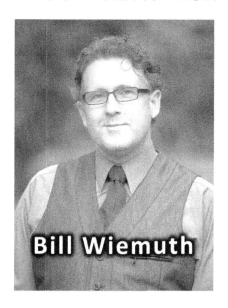

I have loved every moment of my study and sharing of history. In the last two decades, I have proudly written, produced, and published a diverse collection of books, audiobooks, and video presentations which highlight amazing stories from United States history.

As a speaker, I have presented historical stories aboard more than 500 cruises and delivered more than 3,000 presentations for cruise lines and at events across the U.S. and internationally. I also have appeared for numerous regional and national radio television programs including National Public Radio, CNN's "Headline News" and ABC's "Good Morning, America." My collection of 200+ video presentations has been published into its own online streaming video platform.

As a "reporter of the past," I value the skills I learned to earn a B.A. in Journalism from the University of Texas at Arlington. I also have earned an Alaska Naturalist certification from the University of Alaska - Southeast and I have been recognized as a Certified Interpretive Guide by the National Association of Interpretation which provides training for the National Park Service.

Learn more about me and my work to share stories from history, plus enjoy free books, audiobooks, video presentations, a weekly newsletter, and more. Visit us at **HistoryHighlights.com**.

.

Printed in Great Britain
by Amazon